STRENGTHENING THE RANKS

Principles for Effective Team Leadership

By Pastor Mark Cohill

Copyright ©2014 Mark Cohill

Unless otherwise indicated, all scriptural quotations are taken
from the *King James Version* of the Holy Bible. All Hebraic
and Greek definitions are taken from the *Strong's Exhaustive
Concordance*, Baker Book House: Grand Rapids, Michigan

Rivers Publishing Company
P.O. Box 1545, Bolingbrook, IL 60440

ISBN 978-0-9860068-7-6

Printed in the United States of America

ACKNOWLEDGEMENTS

I would first like to thank our Lord and Savior Jesus Christ for the impartation of wisdom and revelation and allowing it to be reciprocated through us to the body of Christ.

To my parents, Sam and Charlene, words cannot express how much you have inspired and encouraged me. I appreciate all of the talks, the funny times, and those home cooked meals. I love you so much, thank you for being my #1 supporter.

To my great leaders Apostle Stephen A. and Prophetess Yolonda Garner. Thank you both for your input into my life, for providing spiritual guidance and entrusting me with the mantle of church leadership.

To my Rivers family, you all are the greatest. I am so blessed to be a part of such a great body of believers. Your prayers, your support, your encouraging words and deeds are so appreciated. I am so proud to be in ministry with such powerful people of God. I love you.

To my graphics and design artist, Laura at www.llpix.com. Thank you so much for taking my vision and creating such a prophetic design for the cover of this book.

To Rivers Publishing, thank you for your patience and your labor of love in formatting and editing this book. I have more coming your way. You Are The Best.

TABLE OF CONTENTS

INTRODUCTION

It is my prayer that this book will help those who serve in leadership in their local church assembly, to bring unity, a spirit of excellence and strength among the ranks of leadership. As leaders it is important to function and operate with a spirit of love, unity, and excellence which is very important to kingdom building. Too often in the church I've encountered a lack of these principles amongst the ranks of leadership, which can weaken an otherwise productive leadership team. I know that there are no perfect people in the world, and the fact of the matter is that we all have flaws, and we will sometimes make mistakes and miss the mark. Thank God for giving us a role model, His son Jesus who was and is the only perfect man to walk in a fleshly body. Jesus knew how to serve both His natural parents and the heavenly Father. He showed us how to serve and love one another. He showed us how to serve and respect those in authority. He also showed us how to build and maintain good character. I pray that this book will encourage and challenge those in leadership to take their act of service in ministry to another level of excellence and strength for the growth and the advancement of the Kingdom of God.

CHAPTER 1

Team Leadership

Let me first define what leadership is. Leadership is the ability of one servant-leader to influence others. It is the ability to inspire others to become who they are in Christ by example. So we should ask ourselves:

1. Am I setting a good example that will inspire others to become who they are in Christ?
2. What is my level of influence?
3. Do I have a genuine love for Gods people?

These are some legitimate questions that will help us to have a general idea of where we are in terms of leadership and our capacity to work responsibly as an individual who's part of a team. God created all of us to lead, we all have leadership capabilities within us, but we cannot lead effectively unless we are filled with the Holy Spirit and led by God's will.

Myles Monroe wrote in his book ***Becoming a Leader****"that there is a difference between The Leader and Leadership, and understanding the two. He said that the leader is the designated position and the individual assuming the position. Leadership on the other hand, is the function of the designated position and the exercise of* *the responsibilities involved in the position.*"Followed by a very true statement, *"there are many individuals who are placed in positions as leaders that fail to provide leadership."* We see it in the corporate world and in the church. In leadership we all work to accomplish a common goal, therefore it is important for us to understand and be clear on the purpose and the vision of our local church assembly. Purpose and vision is the steam and fuel that motivates us in our quest towards the common goal. Jesus knew what His purpose was on earth ;He knew that His goal was to redeem mankind by way of the cross. He was committed to accomplishing the task that was set before Him, although tempted, and persecuted; Jesus still maintained momentum and dedication to the purpose. **Love** and **purpose** was the fuel of His motivation. Maintaining commitment, confidence, and momentum is vital, embrace the vision and work it with everything you got until you see breakthrough.

Working as a team in leadership is important. One person cannot accomplish all of what's involved in ministry, because there are many aspects of ministry that involves much of one's time and attention. Building people, walking with people in their struggles and being sensitive and attentive to God's people alone, is more than enough for one person to handle. There are many area's administratively that require much of one's time also. There is just as much work for those who work behind the scenes as it is for those who work out in the field, but they all work together to accomplish a common goal.

When it comes to ministry, no job is greater than the other. In the New Testament church God established Team Ministry; this is called the Five Fold Ministry. **Ephesians 4:11** gives us a clear understanding of the five-fold ministry. "And he gave some, apostles; and some, prophets; and some, evangelist; and some, pastors and teachers; and in the twelfth verse continues and says "For the perfecting of the saints and for the work of the ministry, for the edifying of the body of Christ." This clearly shows us in verse eleven that God gave these spiritual gifts to the church. These are the God given abilities enabling some Christians to function in these ministry gifts. In verse twelve, God discloses the purpose for this gifted team of individuals; their responsibility is the perfecting of the saints, to train and equip believers to do the work of the ministry. The aim or common goal is for the edifying of the body of Christ, which is to build up the church spiritually.

First, if we are going to function as a good team member, the wise thing for us to do is to examine our own lives to determine what God would have us to do as a member of his team. **Second**, do an inventory often and examine where your priorities should be according to God's word. **Third**, address the overwhelming needs; remember that the need does not constitute the call. The Lord gives us an example in (Mark 1:32-39), the example is simple; we should never use excuses to avoid responsibilities in the things of God.

The one thing to keep in mind is that God has given us all our measure, which is to say that we should allow God to perfect us so that we can function effectively in that measure. I have found that it is less complicated to work with one another when we all operate effectively in our assignments. Remember, God has given you the grace to do what you signed up to do whether it's the ministry of helps, the praise team, or administration, regardless of what capacity you function in you have the grace to operate in it effectively. Imagine every area of leadership within the church operating at its full capacity of measure in excellence, how effective and influential we would be in winning souls and building the Kingdom of God.

Team ministry can be challenging at times simply because we all have our own personalities and come from different back grounds, each of us have experiences and limitations. We even have areas of weaknesses, therefore we are taught that "In the multitude of counselors there is safety."**(Proverbs 11:14)** the one thing we all have in common is our kinship in Christ as brothers and sisters. One can chase a thousand, and two can put ten thousand to flight... **(Deuteronomy32:30)**Working as a strong functional team should reflect similarities that of the divine Trinity. The three persons of the God head are never independent but always work together. In **(Genesis 1:1)** it is shown that God is the initiator of all creation. The second verse shows the Spirit of God hovering over creation. He merely hovers over it as to say He is the protector and the overseer. Finally in the third verse the word of God is the executer of His will. The scripture teaches us the work of the divine Trinity in creation **(Genesis 1:1-2; John 1:1-3; Colossians 1:15-17)**. Thus when a team works together it reflects the creativity that is from God Himself.

We know that two are better than one, if one falls short, the other will lift up his or her brother or sister. It is written in **(Ecclesiastes 4: 9-12)**"But woe to him that is alone when he falleth; for he hath not another to help him up… a three-fold cord is not quickly broken." Our effectiveness is strengthened and we greatly increase in number when we team up. The stronger we are as a team the more we begin to propagate or expand. In ministry we should never act alone, but purpose to always work with a team of counselors. An individual will always go further with a team than alone. Team ministry displays to the world that Christians can work together in unity. The world will know us by our love and unity. Jesus said in **(John 17:21)** "that they all may be as one; Father, art in me, and I in thee, that they may also be one in us: that the world may believe that thou has sent me." God has given us the ability to become unstoppable in our efforts become more effective in our leadership.

Here are four key points that will cause a leadership team to be unstoppable:

1. Being united in the spirit.
2. Having outstanding communication skills.

3. Having a clear vision and goal.
4. Being committed to carrying out the vision and accomplishing the goal.

If a leadership team can possess these points, whatever they set their hands to do in the Spirit, it will be accomplished. This will cause the church to grow effectively in every area of ministry. Let us be committed to maintaining these key points.

When working with a team in most cases members of that team have assigned tasks, duties, or positions. From past experiences I have seen people who were given jobs or assignments just because it needed to be done, and because of this the assignment that was given was deemed ineffective. I am convinced that there should be some form of skill or sensitivity to what is being asked of a person before assigning them to a job. I believe that people should have a motivation, or knowledge of the calling, however sometimes it is necessary I believe, for a person to learn how to function or have some sense of knowledge in other areas of ministry that they may not normally operate in. In leadership we learn to expand our giftedness. I am convinced that it takes a spiritual sensitivity when positioning people into jobs. Remember, this is to help build people, so we must place people in an area where they will be most effective. When I became a member of my church, my Apostle said, "Cohill, find your place and find it quick." I knew exactly what he was saying, and that is my suggestion to you, find your place in the body of Christ, and find it quick, and be fitted into it. Every joint is to supply according to its proper working. We don't have time to sit and twiddle our thumbs wondering what we should do. The church needs everybody in some form or capacity to help advance the Kingdom of God. Wherever God has gifted you, and whatever He has graced you to do find yourself doing it. In most cases the very things that we're strong in and passionate about are the things that we should be doing.

People who have a love and a passion for what they do, have a tendency to do the job more effectively. There are many cases where people are doing jobs because the position looks important and or, it receives a lot of attention. This is an area in team ministry that causes people to become frustrated and angered. This can slow down the productivity of a team which could also affect other areas in the ministry. People waste a considerable amount of time and energy trying to make something happen in an area or position that they are not graced to do. Having a lack of Passion, Love, and Commitment for the assignment are sure signs of someone working in an area outside of what they are really graced for and called to do. This can cause frustration, anger, and bitterness towards others if not dealt with in a timely and Godly manner.

The bible declares that a man's gift makes room for him, and brings him before great men according to **(Proverbs 18:16)** but it is the fruit of the spirit in his life that establishes and maintains his standing in ministry. As leaders it is our responsibility to pay close attention to those we are leading, particularly a person's character, strengths and weaknesses, because who a person is has a lot to do with their purpose. This will help us to identify the gifts and callings of those we are responsible for. I believe that there should be frequent leadership team meetings. The purpose of meetings is to evaluate ourselves personally and evaluate our weaknesses as a team openly so that we can pray, strengthen, and encourage one another. This will also help us to identify and highlight areas of ministry where we fall short and bring a resolve to issues and to ensure that where we missed it won't happen again. I'm a firm believer in preventive maintenance, and meetings are an excellent form of preventive maintenance, it is a simple but effective counter attack for the possibilities of distractions, and spiritual attacks from the enemy.

Teams are very effective in every aspect of life. It began with Jesus when he gathered His disciples and chose twelve, **Simon**, **Andrew**, **James**, (son of Zebedee) **John**, **Phillip**, **Bartholomew**, **Thomas**, **Mathew**, **James**, (son of Alphaeus) **Jude**, **Simon**, (the zealot) and **Judas**. These twelve the Lord designated as Apostles. This was such an important decision that the Lord prayed to God all night concerning this. Jesus appointed these twelve Apostles "that they might be with him and that he might send them out." **(Mark 3:14)**Jesus knew that this team would be with Him throughout His ministry, and throughout this journey, Jesus would pour Himself into their lives with no restrictions. In private, He instilled His plans and His character into these twelve men, He encouraged them. This was the most important team ever assembled and developed to continue on the work of Jesus**(Acts 1:8-9)**. Jesus understood duplicating Himself; He understood that in order to change the world He had to invest heavily in the twelve. Here we are nearly 2,000 years later; we are a living testimony because of Jesus' decision to appoint the twelve.

In the realm of sports we see the example of team work. In football, the running back cannot win the game alone; he needs the blockers, the tight ends and the nose guards to do their job to help him get across the goal line. Even in the corporate world we often hear the terms team player, or team effort. It's teamwork that enables common men to do uncommon things, extraordinary things. The teamwork mentality is another quality of maturity. A team simply put, is a group organized to work together to accomplish a common goal. Team effort is the cooperative effort by the members of a team to achieve a common goal. From a biblical point of view, teamwork means sharing in the biblical responsibilities based on biblical goals, values, priorities, giftedness, training, and Gods leading. Delegation and sharing in responsibilities is very important. When we fail to delegate it causes shortsightedness. Without shared responsibility, we fail to find and develop the potential of others. It causes conceit and fear to manifest. Without delegation and shared responsibilities it causes burnout, we lose our joy and God has called us to serve the Lord with gladness.**(Psalm100:2, Mark 6:30, Exodus18:17-18)**

In my twelve years of servanthood ministry, I have learned in more ways than one what kills church leadership. I read an article by a man named Matt Steen who wrote about this very issue. He wrote *"There are six things that keep church leadership from being healthy,"* or what he calls *Team Killers*:

Over Functioning: Are you or someone in the church leadership doing too much and enabling others (including yourself) to slack off?

Mind Reading: Do you, or does your team, make assumptions about other team members thoughts, agendas, or motivations.

Lack of listening: Can your team listen, truly listen to one another or are conversations merely a group of people talking at one another.

Mistrust: Do you believe your team has your best interest at heart? Do you believe that they have your back?

Lack of Community: Does your team have a sense of community, or are you forced to work with one another.

* Contentment: Are you or your team content with less than or mediocre. Contentment in the Hebrew is (autarkeia), it is a perfect condition of life in which no aid or support is needed, sufficiency of the necessities of life. As a leader our goal should always be to do better.

I believe that these are just a few of many "Team Killers" that infiltrate the church today. With all the information and resources we have available to us today, with God we can take the struggle out of becoming a healthy leadership team.

PRAYER

Father God according to **Proverbs 27:17** Iron sharpeneth Iron so a man sharpeneth the countenance of his friend. I pray for the ability to lead, influence, and inspire others to become who they are in Christ. Father I pray for a genuine love for people so that I may not judge them according to their flaws, but help them see these flaws as opportunities. Father You created us all to lead, so I thank You for the leadership capabilities You put within us to sharpen one another in areas of our lives that will cause us to grow. God let those capabilities now manifest in our lives so that we may effectively lead Your people in our quest toward the common team goal in Jesus name Amen.

CHAPTER 2

Resolving Team Problems

Working as a team is like working with family. We know that with family problems and conflict is inevitable, it can be healthy, or it can be unhealthy. What is unhealthy is unresolved conflict or issues that have been allowed to lay dormant and become a time bomb ready to explode on an otherwise productive team. In Acts 15 we see conflict within and outside the team but in both cases are resolved productively. So how should we deal with conflict?

1. We should pray about the situation alone and ask God to help you discern the reasons behind the conflict, the needs of those involved, and how you may have had a part in it.

2. Keep in mind each other's positions, and listen carefully about each other's views about the situation.

3. Seek possible solutions together and come to a commonality that you both may have in order to accomplish the team goal and see God be glorified.

4. Praying together is a powerful way of seeking agreement. Listen to what God has to say because

He promises peace to His people, His saints. **(Psalm 85:8)**

5. Repent to each other and be rid of any resentment you may still have. Make peace with him.**(Matthew 5:24)**

When in conflict with one another we should ask ourselves, what is important in this situation? What alternative solutions are there? How have I contributed to this situation? We should always examine ourselves first because it very well may be you, unknowingly that may have ignited the conflict.

Here are some scriptures to reflect on:
* Do not seek revenge or bear a grudge against one of your people, but love your neighbor as yourself. I am the Lord." **(Leviticus 19:18)**

* Do not say "I will pay you back for this wrong!" Wait for the Lord and he will deliver you. **(Proverbs 20:22)**

* "Hatred stirs up dissension, but love covers all wrong." **(Proverbs 10:12)**

* "My dear brothers, take note of this, everyone should be quick to listen and slow to speak, and slow to become angry." **(James 1:19)**

* "Tell your people to slander no one, to be peaceable and considerate, and show true humility to all people." **(Titus 3:2)**

When dealing with team conflicts it is of the uttermost importance to have good communication skills. What is communication? Communication is the exchange of thoughts, messages, or information, as by speech, visuals, writing, signals, or behavior. Derived from the Latin word (Communis), meaning to share. Communication requires a sender, a message, and a recipient, although the receivers need not to be present or aware of the sender's intent to communicate at the time of communication. The communication process is only complete when the receiver has understood the message of the sender. Well how does this translate in a church setting? First, leaders must learn to communicate with God and then with others. That order will produce a greater level of effectiveness in our communication.

Communicating effectively is one of the most important skills in life. Effective communication is being able to convey our honest thoughts, feelings, and actions to others in an active listening manner that reflects and glorifies God. This is the foundation of a healthy body of believers. **Inarticulate**, **not listening**, **not expressing** and **not communicating** are the opposites of good communication. These bad characteristics will hinder us from seeking to understand someone, which will lead to misunderstandings, conflict, and strife. God created us as communal people to commune with Him and one another; we must seek and implement good communication in our relationships, and within our churches without prejudice.

We find too often in the church many consultations with others about what to do without first going to God. This is why things don't work out as we hoped, and why we aren't growing as a team and why there are conflicts amongst the ranks. When leaders don't communicate with God first we tend to lean to our own understanding which often leads to conflict. When we trust in Gods guidance it always brings direction and success.**(Proverb3:5-6:14:12)**When we lean and depend on our own strengths and abilities it often causes burn out. Failure to communicate with people properly opens the door for possible misunderstandings which can eventually lead to divisions. As brothers and sisters in Christ we are not and should not be in the business of dividing the team. The bible declares, "And if a house is divided against itself, that house cannot stand." **(Mark3:25)**

The importance of communicating both with God and people cannot be stressed enough. Communication is an on-going, never ending process, and because of that we have to learn to do it better, often, and more effectively. Jesus was and is the master communicator, no other person spoke like Jesus, no other person communicated like Him. Jesus often spoke in parables, but even in the parables the message was clear, it was to the point. Are we communicating like Jesus? Have we really considered how He communicated and are we applying His key aspects?

Here are some aspects of Christ like communication that we should consider in our attempt to communicate more effectively, He was:

*Authoritative
* Aware
* Available
* Attentive
*Approachable

Jesus spoke the heart of the Father. When Jesus had finished speaking, the crowds were amazed at His teaching, because he taught as one who had **authority**, and not as their teachers of the law. **(Matthew7:28-29)**They were amazed at his teaching, because His message had authority. **(Luke 4:31, 32, 36)** While Jesus spoke with authority, He was not an authoritarian forcing people to accept His words. Though all authority belongs to Him, **(Matthew28:18)**, He did not tell people what He knew they needed to hear, but He asked questions, He listened, and He responded. Jesus was aware in His communicating, many accounts in the bible show Jesus addressing the people's needs and concerns before they even spoke.

He had an **awareness** of people's needs that enabled Him to communicate in ways that truly spoke to the moment. He was aware of their thoughts and what was in their hearts. Now in the natural element sometimes we just need to learn to be more observant and develop better listening skills. If we are having difficulties discerning the needs, doubts, fears, concerns, etc. in people; know that as **leaders**, this is an area where we should consistently ask God to develop us in. In the supernatural realm we might say "Jesus is all-knowing, of course He would know peoples thoughts."We should not ever allow that to be our excuse. God has provided us with supernatural resources to help us become more aware with whom we are dealing with and or the situation we are dealing with. This is where the prophetic comes into play. Part of the prophetic is the God given ability to speak ahead of time, what God is about to do, or it can also involve preparing the ground for what God is doing. The prophetic is one supernatural resource that helps us be more aware of the needs of people.

Jesus was **available.** He communicated to the masses yet still found time for the individual. Between His speaking schedule, and His training of the twelve, healing and miracles, He was clear on His purpose. Yet He was not so busy or so intent on meeting His agenda that He didn't have time to communicate with individuals as well as the masses. He also always found time to get away alone to be with the Father. Jesus' availability was unmatched. He was available to answer His disciples' questions and clarify matters for them. He was available to an individual who touched Him even through an entourage of people traveling with Him. He was available to talk with someone calling out to Him for mercy while walking along the road with a crowd of people. Much of Jesus' teaching emphasized the value He placed on taking time for the individual. Jesus cared about both the individual and the masses, and people mattered to Jesus more than task.

Jesus was **attentive.** He actively listened to people's concerns. With all the murmurings from the disciples He could have easily shut them down, but He allowed them to express their concerns before addressing them. Jesus cared about people's feelings He invited and listened to people's opinions. Jesus let people express their needs, even asking them what He could do for them. His attentiveness is significant because Jesus already knew people's concerns, feelings, thoughts, and needs before a word was even spoken. He actively listened to them paying attention not only to their words but also their feelings because people mattered to him. What we should imply as leaders is to pay attention to people well enough to empathize with them. Focus on what people are saying even if you think you know what they are about to say. Listen even when people express disagreement with your ideas or beliefs. Having the Jesus type of attentiveness is having a genuine compassion for people.

Jesus was **approachable.** Though Jesus was born a Jew,

He still engaged in communication with Samaritans and Gentile people. Jesus did not keep to Himself or discriminate between those He would communicate with and those He wouldn't, but He freely communicated with all human beings. He welcomed anyone from sinners to self-righteous religious leaders. These were all people who were far from God. How He communicated varied based on who it was but He still permitted all to come to Him. He communicated with adults as well as children. What we the church should imply in ministry is that **positions** should not separate you from being approachable. Jesus was willing to leave heaven and humble Himself to come to earth on our behalf. Sometimes our perception of a person because of their ministry position may cause us to feel that he or she is not approachable. Pride and your character all play a huge part in being approachable and creating an atmosphere to communicate with people. What can we do to break through preconceived ideas about certain positions in the church?

Prejudices should not define you or separate you from being approachable. Jesus broke through the prejudices and cultural norms. He could be approached by anyone without fear or rejection. This is a huge issue with people who come to church looking for help, counsel, or even salvation and end up leaving because of rejection and leaders not being approachable. If people feel that they can't approach you without being judged, what might you be doing to give that impression? What can you do to break through your own bents and biases to accept all people regardless of who they are or what they've done?

Purpose should not isolate you or keep you from being approachable. Jesus had a specific group to whom He ministered to but still welcomed others to come to Him. A lot of times we find people, leaders, pastors who often say to themselves I'm too busy to deal with that or too busy to talk to this person or that person. I have too much to do or they can wait. WOW!!! If people feel that they can't come to you because you have an agenda that doesn't include them, what might you be doing to give that impression? What can you do to break through a narrow view to get to the big picture perspective of God's overall purpose to love Him and love others? We can all agree that communication is one of the best ways to resolve team problems. Communicating is always in order.

PRAYER

Father God as I pray I ask for Your help to discern the reasons behind conflict. Father I pray for spiritual ears to hear the views of those involved .I pray for wisdom in seeking possible solutions to accomplishing the team goal so that You may be glorified. Father God I ask for a spirit of agreement and peace amongst the team so that we may hear Your voice clearly. God Your word declares in **Psalm85:8**He promises peace to His people, His saints. I thank You Lord for manifesting Your word and Your ways in my life in Jesus name Amen.

CHAPTER 3

Personal Development in Servanthood

What exactly is servanthood? Servanthood is the state, condition, or quality of one who lives as a servant. Further, a servant is first of all one who is under submission to another. For Christians that means submission to God first, and then submission one to another. A servant is one who seeks to meet the real needs of others. Simply put, servanthood is the condition or state of being a servant of ministry to others rather than the service of self, willingly giving of oneself to minister for and to others and to do whatever it takes to accomplish what is best for another. Christ shows that the body of Christ is to function on the basis of servant or servant like ministry to others. Those who are spiritually mature are those who have developed a servant's heart like that of our Lord and savior Jesus Christ. A true concept of mature Christian leadership means serving one's followers and teaching them by example to be servants to others. The true model for mature spirituality and leadership is the Lord Jesus. He spoke of Himself as the Son of man. The contrast between who He was, the Son of man, and what He did, humble Himself, is stressed by the word **"even"** seen in **Mark10:45**, "for **even** the son of man did not come to be served but to serve." Principle: the purpose of serving others is to set them free to love and serve God. We are all responsible to serve one another, but never in order to be served or to satisfy our personal appetites.

Mathew23:11 reads 'The greatest among you will be your servant. '**Matthew 23:12**'and whoever exalts himself will be humbled, and whoever humbles himself will be exalted.' When developing a servanthood mentality the enemy presents many oppositions or hindrances such as **(1) The desire for status or to feel important.** This was an issue among the disciples as seen in **John13**, when we fail to rest in who we are in Christ, we will constantly be fighting the need for importance or significance within our own desires.**(2) A poor concept of one's self worth.** People often seek their self worth from the opinions of others rather than by the value God places on their lives according to His word. **(3) Self centered living.** This naturally results in lack of commitment, wrong priorities, and wrong pursuits which leaves little or no time for the Lord or ministry to others and the body of Christ.

I have found in ministry that the absence of servanthood has become prominent amongst the Christian community or the church as we know it. I have also found that there are consequences in the absence of servanthood such as **(1) Failure to get involved in ministry.** As seen in the disciple's behavior in **John13** the absence of a servant's heart causes people to draw back and expect others to serve them. The attitude is we are here to be ministered to, rather than be empowered and equipped for ministry. **(2) Burnout in those who are ministering**. This can be caused by exhaustion simply because a few people are attempting to do all the work. Burnout can occur because of the pressure and hurt brought on by self-serving motives for acceptance. **(3) Lack of evangelism or lack of ministering to people**. As it reads in Ephesians 4:12 in the equipping of the saints for ministry is the involvement of the whole body in ministry according to the gifts and abilities of the saints. This is a mark of maturity, equipping the saints into mature servants.**(4) The absence of a servant's heart**. This naturally leads to bitterness, contention, and division in the body of Christ. Jesus' style of ministry is the opposite of the world's power based mentality where a man's accomplishments are viewed as a badge of importance and power. Christian love is putting the other person first, seeking the other person's well-being regardless of what it costs us. There is no question that if we as Christians are going to grow and mature into Christ like character, we must experience progress in giving of ourselves in ministry to and for others.

As servant leaders there should be one thing that compels us to act or participate, to serve, and that is **"True Compassion."**God has **True Compassion, John3:16** declares "For God so loved the world that he gave his only begotten son, that whosoever believeth in him should not perish but have everlasting life." Jesus has true compassion, true love. Jesus freely laid down His life for us. Jesus loved us unconditionally; His compassion is what led Him to the cross. To really serve or give of yourself like Jesus did, start with love and compassion. Without love and compassion your servanthood is merely done out of duty. True love and compassion for others is the key to our personal development in servanthood leadership. We must love one another. Here are a few general principles of servant-leadership that will give some direction in your development:

*Listening
Traditionally, leaders have been valued for their communication and decision making skills. Servant leaders must reinforce these important skills by making a deep commitment to listening intently to others. Servant-leaders seek to listen receptively to what is being said and what is not said.

*Empathy
Servant-leaders strive to understand and have compassion for others. People need to be accepted and recognized for their special and unique spirit. One must assume the good intentions of people and not reject them. I have found that sometimes people can have such a critical and judgmental spirit towards one another for whatever reason. Remember we are all God's creation, and He made us just the way He intended. Let us be careful of our perception of others and see one another the way God sees us.

*Awareness
General awareness, and especially self-awareness, strengthens the servant-leader. One must be committed to foster awareness.

*Conceptualization
Servant- leaders seek to nurture their abilities to dream great dreams. Servant- leaders must think beyond day-to-day realities and seek a delicate balance between conceptualization and day-to-day focus.

*Commitment to the growth of people
Servant-leaders believe that people have an intrinsic value beyond their tangible contributions as workers. As such, servant-leaders are deeply committed to the personal, professional, and spiritual growth of each and every individual.

We must not forget, however, the scripture offers a leadership model that should be the cornerstone for leadership within the body of Christ. This biblical brand of leadership is uniquely expressed through what is called "the servant attitude of the leader," the desire to enrich and enhance the lives of those being led through unselfish servanthood. This model of biblical leadership is expressed through an authentic humility that serves others and leads them to become servants as well. **(Matthew23:11-12)**The greatest among you will be your servant. And whoever exalts himself will be humbled, and whoever humbles himself will be exalted.

Character development is very important in our servanthood development. Character is never fully developed because we are always in the process of growing in certain aspects of our character. There are areas of our character that need to be developed adequately for us to perform and function as a servant leader. **Humility** and a **Commitment** to living a Godly life are essential for the growth and development of a servant. Being humble is the way in which we receive Gods grace **(James4:6)**. There is very little to teach someone who lacks true humility **(Psalm25:9)**. The mark of true humility is a teachable spirit. One of the greatest hindrances to service or servant living is the desire for some form of exaltation-position, praise, prestige, and power. Exaltation, praise, prestige, and power are all connected to Pride.

This is where satan lost it, this is why he was kicked out of heaven. **(Luke10:18)** "And he said unto them, I beheld satan as lightning fall from heaven." It was his pride that cost him eternal damnation. What is pride? Pride is having a high opinion of oneself, manifested by demons of arrogance, and haughtiness. Humility and commitment is connected to your character, it speaks volumes to who you really are.**Proverbs22:4** declares **"By humility [and] the fear of the LORD [are] riches, and honor, and life."** What is humility? It is a type of reverence or brokenness we have before God. It is also a modest opinion of who you are. Can humility be developed? Of course, there are many ways to develop humility, here are a few examples:

1. Become as a Child

(Matthew18:2-4) And Jesus called a little child unto him, and set him in the midst of them and said, "Verily I say unto you, except ye be converted, and become as little children, ye shall not enter into the kingdom of heaven Whosoever therefore shall humble himself as this little child, the same is greatest in the kingdom of heaven."

2. Humility is a choice

Whether we have pride or humility it is a choice by the individual that he or she makes. One example is Pharaoh, who chose to be prideful. "And Moses and Aaron came in unto Pharaoh, and said unto him, thus saith the lord God of the Hebrews, how long wilt thou refuse to humble thyself before me."

3. Compelled to be humble

God often allows challenges to enter our lives to compel us to be humble, like the children of Israel:

(Deuteronomy 8:2) And thou shalt remember all the way which the Lord thy God led thee these forty years in the wilderness, to humble thee, and to prove thee, to know what was in thine heart, whether thou wouldest keep his commandments or not.

4. Humility through prayer and faith
Praying to our Father in heaven is also an act of humility. Kneeling in His presence and subjecting ourselves to His will.

5. Humility through fasting
Sacrificing our physical need for sustenance and focusing on our spiritual need. Fasting may seem so difficult but that's what makes it such a powerful tool.

(Psalms35: 13) "But as for me, when they were sick, my clothes was sackcloth: I humbled my soul with fasting; and my prayer returned into mine own bosom."

6. Humility: Fruit of the Spirit
Humility also comes through power of the Holy Ghost. As taught in **(Galatians5:22-23)** three of the fruits are all part of humility:

The bible shows us that there is power in humility. Some people think that being humble is thinking we're no good and others are good, or one who allows people to walk all over them and take advantage of them. That's not Gods picture of humility. In Gods eyes when you are humble you are free from pride and arrogance. Yes in our humanity we know we are inadequate, yet we also know who we are in Christ. Godly humility is being comfortable with who you are in Christ and putting others first.

Do nothing out of selfish ambition or vain conceit, but in humility consider others better than yourselves. **(Philippians2:3)**

As you can see from the following statements that there is power in humility, when you're humble you can defuse arguments and not try to defend yourself all the time. The more you know God the less you have to prove. When you're humble you can handle when people treat you unfair. You can respond without being bitter and without defensiveness.

Let all bitterness, and wrath, and anger, and clamour, and evil speaking, be put away from you with all malice: And be ye kind one to another, tenderhearted, forgiving one another, even as God for Christ's sake hath forgiven you. **(Ephesians4:31-32)**

When God say's to be humble, He lets us know we should examine our motives and attitudes. When you are humble you can talk with the right attitude. You can talk lovingly and kind, regardless of the situation, even when you need to be firm. Remember you are a winner even if you do not win, when you understand Godly humility and put it into practice.

PRAYER

Heavenly Father I thank You for developing a servants heart within me. I ask You Father for a heart of humility that will not allow carnal worldly status, idols of power, position, and prestige to interfere with my service. Lord let the strength of Your humility rest upon my life just as it was upon You when You washed the feet of Your disciples. Father create in me a willingness to serve whole heartedly and not out of duty and self centered motives. Father Your word declares in **Mark 10:45** "For even the son of man did not come to be served but to serve, and to give his life a ransom for many." Father I ask for spiritual eyes, and the gift of seeing to follow You, and see people and the world around us the way You see people and the world. Father grant me grace to be servant hearted and kingdom minded. I depend on Your strength and Your wisdom to serve all mankind with a pure heart and a spirit of love in Jesus name Amen.

CHAPTER 4

Thoughtful Decision Making

As a team player, you will at one point or another be forced to make some decisions, whether simple or tough, bigor small. You may ask yourself, how do I go about making the correct decisions? There are two realities that can be used to base this subject on, **"Scripture** and **Discernment."**Our decision making should be based on what God's word says, and our discernment of a situation and the persons involved. Our discernment and what Gods word says should match, the word of God is our immediate recourse, and the two **"Scripture** and **Discernment"** work together for the perfect solution in decision making. Decision making is an essential leadership skill. If you can learn how to make timely, well-considered decisions, then you can lead your team to a well deserved success. Making team decisions requires a prayerful, thoughtful, intentional, time consuming task of meditation upon God's word and character. Meditation enables us to think and act in accordance with God's character. This is where every decision making process has to start. Our Christian lifestyle is based upon us living, thinking, breathing, eating, and walking out His word. It is with this lifestyle that every decision we make is somewhat guided by God's word. As leaders, our whole life is centered on God's word. We should strive to become more familiar with the word of God and His character, so that spontaneously you think of scriptures, principles, and guidelines that involves or highlights the decision you're making. Here are some direct questions to ask yourself that may help you in your decision making. Will the decisions I make:

>*Help people grow?
>*Help people change?
>*Cause people to reach others?
>*Help people to love better?
>* Produce good results?

Proverbs 3:5-6ESV/Trust in the lord with all your heart, and lean not to your own understanding, in all your ways acknowledge him and he will direct thy paths.

James 1:5ESV/ If any of you lacks wisdom, let him ask God, who gives generously to all without reproach, and it will be given.

John 5:30AMP/ I am able to do nothing from myself (independently, of my own accord- but only as I am taught by God and as I get his orders). Even as I hear, I judge (I decide as I am bidden to decide. As the voice comes to me, so I give a decision), and my judgment is right (just, righteous), because I do not seek or consult my own will (I have no desire to do what is pleasing to myself, my own aim, my own purpose), but only the will of the Father who sent me.

James 3:17KJV/ but the wisdom that is from above is first pure, then peaceable, gentle, and easy to be intreated, full of mercy and good fruits, without partiality, and without hypocrisy.

How many times have you seen a person make a decision based on an emotion or feeling? How often were those decisions wrong? Let's look at the life of Jesus and how he made decisions. We know Jesus was a living human being, a person who never made a bad decision. As a canvas, let us look at the life that Jesus lived.

John 5:19AMP/I assure you most solemnly. I tell you, the Son is able to do nothing of himself; but he is able to do only what He sees the father doing, for whatever the father does is what the Son does in the same way.

John 5:30AMP/ I am able to do nothing from Myself independently, of My own accord- but only as I am taught by God and as I get his orders). Even as I hear, I judge (I decide as I am bidden to decide. As the voice comes to me, so I give a decision), and my judgment is right just, righteous), because I do not seek or consult My own will (I have no desire to do what is pleasing to Myself, My own aim, My own purpose) but only the will and pleasure of the Father who sent me.

John 8:28-29AMP/So Jesus added, When you have lifted up the Son of Man (on the cross), you will realize (know, understand) that I am He (for whom you look) and that I do nothing of Myself (of My own accord, or on My own authority), but I say (exactly) what My father has taught Me.

John 12:49-50 AMP/ This is because I have never spoken on My own authority or of My own accord or as self appointed, but the Father who sent Me has himself given Me orders (Concerning) what to say and what to tell. And I know that his commandment is eternal life. So whatever I speak I am saying (exactly) what My father has told me to say in accordance with his instructions.

John 7:16; 10:25;14:10; 17:7 AMP/Jesus made decisions in life based on the desires of the Father, therefore, all of the actions of Jesus are said to be true. Everything that Jesus did have the highest spiritual and moral quality. Jesus being fully human experienced the full spectrum of emotions and feelings that we have experienced. As a man Jesus lived a life of absolute dependence on His Father. He knew that trying to accomplish the Fathers will on His own would not work. Everything He did was at God's instructions. Our job is to acknowledge God in all we do and let Him lead us... all the time. You can be sure that when making decisions, you will not be off course when you begin at the acknowledge point, making sure that we always seek God first. That's the place we should live, at all times. If we don't start right we won't end right. Jesus was always in constant communication with God, He lived a life looking into the heavens, listening to the Father. Jesus, without ceasing, watched and listened for every instruction from the Father, and did everything He saw and heard from Him with no resistance. Just simply listening and obeying God is the rule of thumb in making thoughtful decisions. We are to do the exact the same thing to make the right decisions, we must be unceasingly looking and listening to our Father, through His word and prayer; and the do what He directs us to do. One of the main reasons Jesus always made the right decisions is that there was purity in His motives. There was no breach to His spirit with selfish desires, fame or reputation, comfort, or self glory. It was all about what God the Father desired. I believe that when we begin to have a heart and a pure desire like that of Jesus, we will begin to see people and the world differently. When this happens it will change our whole perspective of serving Gods people.

At some point in our lives we will be faced with making important decisions in the upcoming years, decisions that will affect our families, our jobs, and so forth. However we must be careful not to helplessly fall into a trap by using a process of making decisions that may not be biblical. After doing some research I have found that there are at least two methods most people use in making decisions today. The first method is the **"Pro and Con method."** This is a system that is used by separating the two and determining which one makes the most logical sense. The second method is **"The Outcome Method."** In other words how will the decision affect us? Some may be guilty of using this method, driven by outcome versus what is right according to what God is saying. Yes these methods do play a part in the process of making a decision, but they should not be the determining factors. Making decisions based on biblical and Christian beliefs can be a challenge for many Christians. For some we operate out of what we call **"learned behavior, "**when we have been doing things so long in our own strength and our own understanding, when we are challenged by God to begin to operate according to His word our flesh wants to rebel because of "**Learned behavior."**

Before making tough decisions we should always consecrate ourselves in prayer. Never attempt to make any decision great (or small) until you have prayed about it. Take for example Jesus, in **Mark14:34** Jesus was face to face with making the toughest decision of his life. He wrestled with the outcome and said... "Father remove this cup from me." The decision Jesus made to die for our sins was a tough one but necessary. As overwhelming as the opposition was He made the decision and died with it. Tough decisions are ones that you must be willing live and die with let's take the three Hebrew boys for example. Shadrach, Meshach, and Abednego, in the book of **Daniel chapters1-3,** these three men were known for their exclusive devotion to God. They were thrown into a fiery furnace by king Nebuchadnezzar because they refused to worship the gods he worshiped and bow down to his golden image. Because they made a tough decision to stand for what they believed and whom they believed in, and to live and die by it, God came in the midst of them in the fiery furnace, and delivered them and the bible says that they were not consumed. When we make decisions based on Christian principles, precepts, and biblical truth, it will ultimately bring glory to God.

Let us look at another great example, Daniel, who was a trustworthy man whom God had given the gift of interpretation of dreams. King Darius had issued a decree that for 30 days no one was to pray to any gods or man other than himself. When Daniel heard about the decree he went to his home and prayed. The bible says that Daniel went to his window that overlooked Jerusalem and kneeled and prayed to God three times a day, so he was accustomed to this. Because of this, king Darius had thrown Daniel into the lions den. However in the midst of this Daniel made the decision that he would not let anything stop him or sway him from his commitment to God. Because of this the bible says that God sent an angel and shut the mouths of the lions and Daniel was not harmed. These are some instances where real people in tough situations who had to make tough decisions and were willing to live and die by them. God never promises that making decisions will be easy... so don't let difficult circumstances, people, places, or events stand in the way of sticking to God honoring decisions. Sometimes the most difficult choices in life are not those between wrong and right, but choices of what is good and what is best. Each of us needs to listen to our hearts and the prompting of the Holy Spirit to know what things God would have us to do. Just because something may not be wrong, does not mean that it is right for you at this time in this situation. If we are spending time in the word of God and acting on His advice, we will consistently make good decisions. **Hebrews 5:14 NLT** says **"Solid Food is for those who are mature, who have trained themselves to recognize the difference between right and wrong and then do what is right."**

As you go about life day today and week by week, in your decision making, remember that we live under grace and compassion, but in all things strive to be like the One who created us all, Jesus Christ our Lord and Savior.

PRAYER

Prayer for Godly Thoughtful Decision Making

Father I thank you for the grace to make Godly decisions according to Your word. Father I pray **John 5:19 AMP/ I assure you most solemnly. I tell you, the son is able to do nothing of himself; but He is able to do only what He sees the father doing, for whatever the father does is what the son does the same way.** Father I pray for supernatural strength and boldness to make difficult decisions in tough situations. Father my hope and my trust is in You. I totally submit my mind and my heart to Your will. Father I decree that the decisions I make will be based on Your word and the leading of Your Holy Spirit. I come out of agreement with all sprits of selfish pride that will cause me to make wrong decisions based on personal or emotional influence. Father I thank You for a greater sensitivity to the leading of Your Holy Spirit, and I thank You Father that I lean not to my own understanding but only to the wisdom of Your Holy word in Jesus name Amen.

ABOUT THE AUTHOR

Mark Cohill was born and raised in Gary Indiana. A huge part of his upbringing has always been in the church. Mark had his start in church leadership at an young age. As he grew and matured in his faith walk he was ordained as an elder. It was then when Mark noticed that he had a heart to serve. Serving became his passion which developed an anointing and a grace to inspire leaders or those assigned to work in various areas of ministry to operate at a greater level of excellence. Presently as a Pastor under the leadership of Apostle Stephen A. Garner he has the responsibility and charge to Shepherd, and equip the sheep for further kingdom advancement.

CONTACT INFORMATION

PASTOR MARK COHILL

EMAIL: maccdc.mc@gmail.com

www.ingramcontent.com/pod-product-compliance
Lightning Source LLC
Chambersburg PA
CBHW072038060426
42449CB00010BA/2326